What the Abenaki Say About Dogs

... and other poems and stories of Lake Champlain

Dan Close

The Tamarac Press • Warren, Vermont

2009

Cover illustration by Jennifer Salmon

Use of the Vermont Celebrates Champlain logo on
back cover courtesy of the Vermont Lake Champlain
Quadricentennial Commission

ISBN 978-0-9706620-1-9

The Tamarac Press, Warren, Vermont

This book is dedicated to the memory of
Wolfsong,
A Native American storyteller and scholar
Born April 25, 1953   Passed over, November 24, 2000

CONTENTS

How This Book Came To Be

Some years ago, the Abenaki of northwestern Vermont staged a demonstration against the practices of certain homebuilders who were placing homes on sites the Abenaki had identified as ancient burial grounds of their people. About a month after that demonstration, I happened to be near the area in question, and I decided to see just what it was they were talking about. I drove down a rural road to a spot that had been set aside to commemorate the first Christian church ever erected in what is now Vermont. It had been built as a mission church by Jesuits from Canada back in 1700 AD.

Along the way, I noticed a small group of people standing around a big yellow loader parked on a small building lot. The lot had been ripped up by someone who had begun to dig a cellar hole and then stopped. The loader's scoop, filled with sand, had been lifted to table height. The people standing around it didn't look like the usual work crew. There were four of them: two men and two women. They looked at me with more than usual interest as I passed by, which I found somewhat disquieting.

Their interest piqued my interest, so after I had visited the small commemorative area for the church, I stopped at the excavation site on my way back. One of the women came over to my car and introduced herself as Donna Moody, the Repatriations Coordinator of the Western Abenaki. She explained that it was her duty to locate the bones of the Abenaki ancestors and save them from destruction and desecration. "This is where a builder started to dig up a graveyard," she said, "until we got a court order to stop him." She told me that they were scooping up the disturbed soil and sifting through it, looking for the bones of their ancestors. The scene was imbued with solemnity of the highest order.

I told her that I did not wish to intrude, but that I felt I had to stop and let them know what I was doing there since they had seemed somewhat apprehensive when I passed them before. Donna immediately put me at ease and said that it was good that I was there; it was good that I could see what they were doing.

Meanwhile, my little cocker spaniel, Buffie, who had been sitting in the passenger seat, climbed onto my lap and stuck her head out the window to say hello to Donna. It was love at first sight for both of them. After a long time of meeting and greeting and talking between the two of them, Donna looked at me smiling and said, "Do you know what the Abenaki say about dogs?" I did not know, and so she told me the story.

I drove off down the road for maybe a mile and I pulled off to the side and wrote this poem: What The Abenaki Say About Dogs. Wrote it right out.

I might have changed a word or two later on, but it was just
one of those things that comes to you by itself, right out of
the air. I sent a copy of it to Donna, along with another poem
I called Sifters.

These poems led to others over the years, and this book
is the result of my regard for the Abenaki – their culture,
their history, their place in contemporary society, and their
traditional dwelling places in the mountains and especially
along the shores of this great lake called Champlain or as the
Abenakis call it, The Sea Between.

I do not pretend to speak for The People of the Dawn. They
are entirely capable of speaking for themselves, and have a
great and long tradition of poets and singers and storytellers
you can go to for their work. This book speaks of their
interaction with the land and this great inland sea. I simply
hope that here in this small volume I have done them justice.

Dan Close
Underhill, Vermont
2009

WHAT THE ABENAKI SAY ABOUT DOGS

THE ABENAKI SAY THIS:
WHEN YOU PASS OVER
TO THE NEXT ABODE,
YOU RISE FROM YOUR DREAM
AND WALK THROUGH THE FOREST.
A LONG TRAIL YOU WALK.
IT IS PLEASANT, WITH TREES
THAT RISE ABOVE YOU
AND LEAVES AND MOSS
SOFT BENEATH YOUR MOCCASINS.
THEN YOU COME TO A RIVER.

OVER THE RIVER THERE IS A BRIDGE.
ON THE BRIDGE STAND ALL THE DOGS
YOU HAVE EVER KNOWN IN YOUR LIFE.
IF YOU HAVE TREATED THEM WELL
THEY GREET YOU AS THEY HAVE IN LIFE
AND WALK WITH YOU ACROSS THE BRIDGE
INTO THE LIGHT OF THE NEXT LIFE.

IF YOU HAVE NOT TREATED THEM WELL,
YOU WILL NEVER CROSS THAT BRIDGE.

MAQUAN

Maquan, the woman who touches
>   the essence of things the Manitou has made,
Touches our arms, the insides of our palms,
>   the insides of our eyes.

She makes us feel and see
>   with the lightness of a bird's feather
The heavyness of history
>   before humankind was born.

So then too she makes the frogs sing
>   in the heavy rain and the light mist.
The breath of life rises in the air.
>   The salamanders swim, as do the perch,
Over the bright yellow sand
>   beneath the silently gliding canoe.

INDIAN COUNTRY

I sit in my camp by the shore of the lake

    and watch the sun rise in the quiet of the dawn.

I have watched this lake in summer and winter;

    in fall and spring I have watched.

Through all the seasons and over many years

    I have watched.

Now it is summer again – high, hot summer,

This morning a mist hung over the lake

    from the torrents of rain and

    the clash of lightning that came

    last night in the evening

    and all through the night until

    just before dawn.

And the sun barely broke through the mist,

    coming like a god's red fireball.

Yesterday I watched the thunderstorms

    as they marched across the sky

driving the lightning before them

from west to east, from north to south –

giant forks of lightning pitchforking down

upon the green hills to the east,

frothing the waters of the lake into great waves,

and once,

when the air changed,

a wall of wind blew down the water from the north

and lifted the tops off the waves

turned them into a frenzied fine spray

that blew by itself, racing across the fractured waters

heading south

to no one knows where.

Perhaps somewhere in the south some fisherman

looked up from a sandbar into the spume

and thought it was rain.

Oh but here I am again

back in Indian Country

back in the Indian Country of the heart.

Oh to be an Indian again!

I sit in my camp and think of Indians

    who sat on this spot so many years ago

    old Indians who sat with grandchildren

    and showed them thunderstorms that came then

    shoving and power-paddling their black and

    purple clouds across the lake

    and telling the babies of Gloosgap and the Thunderbird

    how Gloosgap threw giant rocks into the lake to make

    the islands; how the great Thunderbird flys

    the lightning across the skies

And I would watch the children's eyes open wide with

    wonder at my tales.

That is the gift I could give them.

Here among the great cedars by the lake

    along the shale beaches, among the birds and bears

    and deer and the mighty fish of the lake

    I could show them. Once again, I could show them

    what it is to be Indian, to be the great hunter,

    to live in Indian Country.

SUNSET VIEW WEST FROM CHAMPLAIN

Gods there were on those heights
In the earliest of days

After the rains came down on the bare earth
And divided the land from the sea

Gods there were on the bare rocks
Of the highest hills

And they stood, their heads held higher than the heavens,
their feet planted firm within the rock

When the earth was wide
before the green trees and
grasses and sedges
grew upon the land

Before the mosses came,
and the willows and poplars,
before the animals and fish, and the stars,

The Gods stood on their mountaintops

and they danced

Swinging their warclubs and lances high,

Their heads thrown back against the sky,

Throats wide open,

Shouting out the names of men and women

yet to come,

And screaming out their deeds

In pasts and futures yet to be

That is what we hear in the howling winds of winter,

In the lightning of the summer,

That is what we see in the thunderheads amassing

fury in the orange glowing of the setting sun —

echoes of gods that There Be . . .

THE HEAD OF LAND

Beyond the head of land

The multi-nationed fishermen still stand up straight

In their motorboats,

Trolling motors on quiet,

And they wait.

Old muskie sits down under

In his green embankment.

He waits, too.

And the summer sun rises and falls,

The air charged with orange early and late,

Then sudden silver dusk.

Small sounds of slaps and chugs across the waters,

And Moon comes up, red and full with the close-to-earth air,

Then later, silver-bright.

Over the bight the wild loon sings,

And the whole night turns silver.

Dark trees shadow-shape laughing ripples underneath the

shore,

Create monsters, angels, spirits, muskums, elves.

The bright bird sings,

And on the land

Eyes like meteors pierce the night.

Our bones are made of the earth;
The earth is made of our bones.
~ Wolfsong ~

SIFTERS

Under all is the land.

Down through the years,

Under all the rights that move and shift,

That are born and are extinguished

By the say-so of a new nation,

By the sing-song of judicial determination,

All the while,

Under all is the land.

Always the land grows smaller.

This parcel, now, that sits on a hill

Overlooking the Mississquoi River,

Destined to be a homesite for some person ~

Here, now, sits a grand example

Of sing-song determination,

Of the say-so of a new nation.

Not a hundred yards away there stands a monument

To a church built by the Jesuits

To sanctify the heathen Abenak

Three hundred years ago.

First church in Vermont, they say.

Just the monument remains.

No church. No Abenak. Nothing more.

Ah, but wait!

Under church, under missing steeple,

Under the nearby residential parcel

Under all is the land,

And the land is filled with bones.

Under all the bundles of rights that the builder

       has purchased from someone

       who never owned the land

       who bought it from some other who

       had never owned the land

All the way back to a man who had

       leased the land for a hundred years

       from Abenaks who marked their x's

         and then died,

Under all of that lie the dead of the land,

the dead of the clan, the dead of the band,

the dead of the Abenak nation

       who granted the leases

          that somehow never ended,

            and the land increases.

The bulldozer comes and rips up the land ~

Sod, topsoil, rock, clay, humus, red dirt, sand ~

And from under the ripped-up land come bones,

      trinkets, a bronze statue of Christ,

And bits and pieces of great-grandparents,

   long-ago-dead babies,

     scarred warrior bones,

       stretched mothers' bones,

old bones, new old bones, scattered to the air,

Lifted out of there,

All for the sake of a new house by the river.

Pleasant place, that riverside lot

    full of bones ...

They walk slowly, reverently, over the ground.

Over this place that was to be for some person's house,

Over this graveyard of the dead.

Lovingly they turn the earth,

These gleaners, these sifters, these nowaday children of

         the Abenak.

Here on the high bank above the Mississquoi

Where the bulldozer has roared,

Where the backhoe has ripped,

They kneel or stand like ghosts,

And let the topsoil, red dirt, sand

Slip through their fingers.

Now they are come

To look for the bones ~

The bones of their ancestors are here,

Glistening, under their rubbed-in coats

> *of dusky dirt.*

Here are the brittle bones

The saved bones

Gently they raise them up,

Crooning love songs, they save them.

When the looking is finished,

> *they will put them back where they belong,*

> *praying that they will be undisturbed forever.*

Now, who can say who owns this land?

Can the judge say?

Can the review board say?

Can the living say?

The dead can say:

> We own this land.
>
> We live in this land.
>
> We live here forever.
>
> Leave us in peace.

And today, the young ones, living,

Sift through the earth

Searching for bones

To give the bones back to the earth.

To give the bones back to the ancestors.

What has any law to do with this?

These bones have rights beyond the laws of men.

Leave them alone. They have earned their rest.

THE SACHEM OF SUNFLOWERS

In the fullness of Autumn
In the flower of harvest time
I saw the Sachem of Sunflowers
Standing in the midst of his clan
Along a country road in Jericho.

My heart, my mind, stopped time
Held it
Held the vision ~
A country garden
Underneath the sun
Beneath the clairvoyant blue sky
Of a snappy North Country day.

There he stood
Full and mature
Head bent away from the sun,
Looking down at the earth from which he sprang
        and flourished for a long summer season
His dark rich leaves, hunched around and over him
        like a cloak,

Dark green, and great with life

He bent his yellowed head to bless the earth.

Around him all his band,

Left and right, he the tallest,

All bending toward him,

Following his gaze.

That bright, benevolent head;

That staff he leaned upon;

That cloak of leaves; that prime full green

That maned this lion of the sun ~

Such instances in time

Are what make magic.

Worlds hurtle by

Each in its own delight,

But no time stops for any man

Unless that man takes time

To see the magic in the earth and sky.

If we but stop to see

We'll find the dream

We tramp along through time

Seeking to find,

Seeking to be.

BRIGHT STAR

I was so happy that year,

when we spent the summer on the southern isle.

Every day we watched the sun rise.

Seated on the top of the cliff

next to the rough-barked cedars

we looked out over the Inland Sea,

our arms around each other;

And every morning I put my hands on your belly

    to measure it.

Then we would sit and laugh

    and have contests, just the two of us,

    and bet on when the baby would be born.

At the end of July it was.

On a morning fresh with the beads of dew, I, waking early,

    saw Orion ranging over the horizon to the east,

        along with the pre-dawn light.

Stealthily, with no noise, I picked up my shotgun and bow

    and crossed in my moccasins away across the land.

Beyond our campsite, far away,

I sat beneath a maple tree on the side of a field,

and waited.

Silence. An hour's wait. Silence.

Just at the edge of daybreak

an old Tom Toddler tippled into the field,

falling out of some sumac scrub.

He went about his business

rooting away for all he was worth,

coming towards me,

and I,

I blasted him.

Picked him up by the neck.

Carried him home,

Lifted up the blanket

that was the door to our tent,

And I stood there, silent and amazed.

You were turned away from me.

Naked, you knelt on bunched blankets,

your black hair cascading down your ivory back,

and when you heard me enter at the door

you turned your head

and with a smile, said,

"While you were away, she came."

I will take the curve of your mouth,

Your smile, your gleaming eyes,

     forever with me.

To my grave, I will take the beauty of you

     on that day, with me.

Every day I wake, I will take the look of you

     on that day, with me.

"See," you said, and turned around to me, smiling.

At your breast was a delicate thing

with delicate lips, and delicate fingers,

and bright black eyes.

"Aiyee!" I said softly.

I saw your questioning lips, and then you whispered,

"Come look." You stopped, and looked at me,

     and smiled again, and said,

"But leave the turkey outside."

I looked down.

I, great hunter, had brought you a dead turkey,

with eXes for eyes, and buckshot aplenty

in his wings and breasts and thighs.

And while I was about that,

You brought me an angel.

How is that?

Am I not the great provider?

Am I not the great hunter?

So how did you deliver this bright beauty?

All alone, how did you do this

while I was out sitting under a tree

in the still dimness of the green dawn?

"What can I do?" I asked, and knew

there was nothing I could do.

"Be happy," you said.

"There must be something I can do," I said.

"Bring me a pot," you said. "I will need strength.

We will make a soup out of your buckshot turkey."

"I do not know how to . . . ," I said.

"Oh, I will do it," you said,

". . . and you will pluck the feathers."

"I?" said I.

"Aye," you said.

"And what shall we call this miracle?" I asked.

"She came just before dawn," you said,

"She came with the morning star.

"We should call her, Bright Star."

"That is good," I said.

"Build up the fire and start the soup," you said.

I knelt, hand upon your strong young back, and
watched Bright Star. She went to your
nipple, mewed, sucked, drank in your milk,
drank in the summer day.

Outside, birds sang.
Waves splashed against the shore.
A quiet morning.
No other sound.

THE YOUNGEST PRIEST TALKS TO THE SPIRIT OF THE WATERS

Come at last to the edge of the lake,
I splash the water with my hand,
Dispel my tired visage
Break it into waves and dreams
And then I dip my head
And drink.

The water is sweet;
Mild in the August of my life.
Finally I have found
What I have sought
Since the sun first broke upon my eyes.

So long a search!
Now I can drink and be quiet in my mind.
Now I can bring back what is mine,
What I have found,
What is the universe to me.

Now I can not just look,
But feel, encompass,
Show you,
See!

The clouds are white.

The lake is blue.

The reeds along the shore

Skirr with the music of the air.

It is for me to explore.

I have found my home.

The universe expands

to accommodate my small infinity.

THE ALBURG AUCTION HOUSE

Reason I like the Alburg Auction House on a
    Saturday auction night is,
I run into lots of people I know.
And if you don't like what's on auction,
You can always go outside where you'll always find
A bunch of the boys, and you can have a good talk
    about engines and boats and trucks and
    backhoes and where the fish are biting,
And along toward the end of the night
You can hear the same old story
    about Clarke Dodge's deer,
    the one he saw at dusk one year
    and never got a bead on
    but it was 508 pounds and 22 points
    and still growin', last I heard,
    and it's still out there for the takin'.

But if you stay inside, you can have a good time, too,
    watchin' the crowd havin' a good time
    doin' foolish things like bidding on mystery boxes
    and pawing through whatever junk's inside,
    and sometimes there's treasure in there.

Fun to bid a dollar on something you've decided
        all of a sudden you've gotta have or bust.
I've done it too. Price of admission.
        You watch them. They watch you.
        Good easy fun on a Saturday night.
        The kids like it, burrowin' through that stuff.

The auction stuff is up on the stage.
The audience sits in rows of attached chairs
        that the auctioneers, the Benedict brothers,
        took out of some church or school
        some time ago, found useful, so they kept,
        and for a good price too, I betcha.

So Charlie Benedict is up on stage,
His draggers dragging things to the front,
Holding them up high so everyone can see,
And Charlie's singing out his song:

        "Hey whatamibid for ringading ding ding ding ding dang
            Hey rangadang dang dang dang dang ding."
Like a talkin' cash register
and all of us responding with Yups and
Yeps and raised fists and signs and
winks and signals and laughs and

Charlie is going "ring a ding ding dang I've got

twenty-five who says thirty ca-ching ding ding ding . . ."

And on into the night,

and I tire of it a bit

so I leave my wife sitting there

and go out back by the indoor hot dog stand,

sort of like being in church: You know,

standing in back behind the seats,

lined up on the back wall with all the other miscreants,

in there but not really there,

observing, but not a communicant, for the

time being, at least,

and I light up my pipe and stand there,

lookin'.

After a few minutes I sort of feel something

to my right, a presence of some sort,

and I turn just a bit, take a puff and

let it out, and look, and there's

Old Jack standing there, lighting up his pipe too,

and puffin' slow as the world was born. He nods,

between puffs.

"Why, say, Jack," I say. "Haven't seen you all winter. How
    you been?"

"Not too bad," says Jack. "You?"

"Not too bad. How's the family?"

"She's down there, in the center." He nods toward the
    middle of the room, his baseball cap pointing the way
    like a boat's prow through the bay. "Kid's with her there."

I look. I see her and the kid.

"Well, you got that right," I say. "There they are."

"She's got her eye on a vacuum cleaner," says Jack. "That
    little one on the right of the stage. Kind of red;
    maroon. Looks like Artoo-Deetoo? She says it works good."

"What do you think?" I ask.

"I think she says it works good," says Jack. "She's
    the one gonna use it. What d'I kayare?"
    he asks in a real twangy way out of his nose.
    "Damn thing is noisy enough."

"Good for camp, maybe," I say.

"Good for the truck," says Jack, "after my dog's been in it."

"How's the boy?" I ask, knowing, like everyone else in town,
    that his boy's been havin' trouble in school.

Jack snorts and says, "He's been havin' a bit of trouble

in school. Can't read yet. Can't pay attention.

They're all worried."

I look down into the crowd. There's Tina, Jack's wife,

and next to her there's Sandy, the boy, or his head,

just the top of it, sticking out over the back of his chair.

"They sent him to a state agency down to Burlington, to see

what's wrong with him," says Jack.

Well, I don't say anything. There's some things

you just don't ask about. The other fellow's

got to tell you if he wants. Jack wants to tell.

It's bothering him.

"So he goes to the agency, him and his mother, and

they sit and talk and have interviews with

all kinds of people all day long, and then some

young lady takes him into her office and she

says to him, 'Well, Sandy, can I ask you some

questions?' 'Sure,' says Sandy. He's always up

for a good talk, y'know. So she asks him

his name and address, and a few other things,

stuff an eight-year-old would likely know,

and then she says, 'Well, now, Sandy,

can you tell me, what are the four seasons?'"

Jack looks at me and sort of snorts and says,

"So Sandy says to her, smarter-n-hell,

'Trout, squirrel, coon, and deer.'"

Then Jack laughs, and says,

"So the young lady looks at him, Sandy says,

and stops askin' questions. She just looks at him

like he's from another planet or somethin',

and Sandy says to her, 'What's the matter?

Didn't I get them right?' and the lady's eyes

light up, he says. I think he likes her, the way

he talks about her."

Jack draws on his pipe and says, "So her eyes light up,

and she covers her mouth with her hands,

then she takes them down and she says,

'Oh, no, Sandy. You got them just right. Now,

would you sit there for a minute or two? I have

to go talk to some people, and then I'll be right back.'"

"So the young lady leaves, and Sandy sits there, waitin'
and wonderin', and sure enough she comes back.
She's gone and got Tina, and right in front of Sandy,
and she's got her hand on Sandy's shoulder, she
likes him, too, I think, she says to Tina, 'Mrs. Benay,
there's nothing wrong with your boy.' Well, there's a
sigh of relief out of Tina, and there's Tina and Sandy
feeling good, and the young lady continues. 'We've
given him all kinds of tests, and he's normal. It's just that...'
and she stops, then says, 'Well, it's a cultural thing, Mrs.
Benay. I asked him to name the seasons, and he said
trout, squirrel, coon, and deer. Those aren't the answers
the test wanted, but he's right. If he's lived with knowing
those seasons, he's right. He just doesn't know what the
test wants him to say. That's what's happening to him.'

'That's his dumb father talking to him,' says Tina. 'Always
talkin' about deer season.'

'Grandpa told them to me,' pipes up Sandy.

'See, that's what I mean,' says the young lady. 'If he's been
living those seasons all his life, and that's what's right

from what he sees, why should he give any other answers? Why should he learn to read, for that matter? He doesn't see any use for it. He has to see a use for it before he'll want to do it. You'll have to tell him why he wants to read.'

Jack takes a break and tamps down the ashes in the bowl of his pipe. "What do you say to that, Medicine Man?" he asks.

Well, I know that Sandy's hidden name is Sand Speaker, because he always sits on the beach alone and talks to the wind. And I know that the boy's grandfather knows a lot of the old ways, and I can see him running on to Sandy at length about them.

"Hell," says Jack. "Sure I tell him about deer season. But I tell him too he has to get something to do with his life. I say that he should do like I did, get my CDL. Best thing I ever did. Let's me drive across country any time I want, and get back here for Deer Season . . ."

"And Pike-shootin' Season, and Ice-fishin' Season, and as many of the others as you want," I say.

"Well, what the hell do the schools know about that?" Jack
wants to know.

I turn to him. "I think the state was right," I say. "He won't learn to
read until he wants to. It's up to him. Meanwhile, just have fun
with him. You know how much he really knows."

"Yeah," says Jack. His body straightens. "I'm amazed at how much he
knows. I just gotta be sure he knows how much he knows."

"That's right," I say. "It'll all come out real good some day. You'll see."

"Whaddimibid bid bid bid bid," goes on Charlie Benedict.
"Whaddimi ding ding ding ding ding
ding ding ca-ching ding ding ding ding dang . . ."

SUMMER LAKE EVENING

When the mist comes down on the water
  After the hot storms of summer have
    blown across the sky,
  The lake shrugs on its deep color of slate
  The sky slate-colored too with cloud.

    On an evening like this
  With small rough waves splashing
    like the clatter of knives
    against the shore,
  The heron croaks like a pterodactyl.

 With the clouds low down
    and the air shifting and heavy,
    the hills obscured except for the shores,
  Then it is that the world goes flat,
  Spreads out as far as any eye can see
  And it could be any year
  Any sea
  Any inlet
  Any ocean.

Ocean.

The lake can still be that
Even now, even still,
Even land-locked now amid its green
          and ochre hills.
I can feel that once upon a time
Ocean was here; Lake was Ocean.

I can almost smell it.
On an evening like this ~
The soft, heavy breath of the sea.
The hissing waves lie swelling almost flat;
The soft, heavy breath of the sea . . .

It is there

Sky undecipherable

The eagle's wings whisper

THE BOLD MACGREGOR

It was late July, on a midsummer night lit by a half-moon that glinted and gleamed off the surface of the wide lake. Small waves lapped at the shale beach below MacGregor's deck, and along the shore, light breezes set the narrow, toothed leaves of the willows whispering. High up in the sky to the west, huge cumulous clouds that would be dangerous on a hot summer afternoon floated placidly over the massive black ranges of the Adirondacks. They lumbered and tumbled together like an armada of galumphious cabin cruisers, constantly changing their shape in the moon-lit sky.

It was fitting, thought MacGregor, that those sights and sounds set the rhythm of the night. The leaves, the waves, the moon . . . all together made the night, along with the shades of purple and deep, deep blue, and the fainter twinkle of the stars that competed with the moonlight and the billowing clouds so high above. Altogether a fine feast for the eye and the ear, and for the mind as well. Here on the shore of Arnold Bay, the view west across the expanse of Lake Champlain was magnificent in daylight or at sunset, or at dawn, or as now, at almost midnight. It was the peace that had brought him to this spot. Here he owned a beautiful lake house, and the deck that stretched

westerly from its back doors to the water gave him a view of
the far shore and the Adirondack ranges as they built up and
up, one after another, four or five deep. Those ranges seemed
to go on and on forever, luring the soul of the watcher farther
and farther toward the west. So did the sky invite adventure,
and so did the lake, the lake especially, for although this was not
its widest point, only some five miles here, it could be wild and
wide enough to cause trouble when it wanted to and the wind
blew from the right direction. Or it could bring a serene, special
calmness to the earth just as it was doing right now.

MacGregor owned almost two thousand feet of lakeshore,
a third of a mile on the lake, and those two thousand feet of
frontage extended in a block back from the shore to the road
a couple of thousand feet as well. His driveway started at the
three-car garage next to the house and headed east toward the
road. It meandered through the cedar forest that surrounded the
house, straightened as it dived along one side of a wide pasture,
plunged into yet another small forest, and finally emerged onto
the town road, looking for all the world like a little lane that led
nowhere. Not many casual viewers would guess that at the other
end of that little lane were the garage and the barn and the guest
house and the nearly four thousand square foot main house
perched on its low bluff overlooking the water.

And that's exactly how MacGregor wanted it. He was seventy-eight, and he wanted the privacy and the solace the land and the lake brought whenever he was of a mind to have it. He was not a recluse. He was, in fact, pretty active. He was tall and thin and wiry in a way that could look mean at times, and the meanness could extend to his jaw line when it had to, as it had a few too many times in the past in any number of business transactions. But there was a softness to his stern visage as well, a softness that was reserved for family and friends.

He had lived an active life. He was always a tinkerer from as far back as he could remember. He went to engineering school much more from curiosity than simply for searching out a career. In business, he developed a number of inventions and had done so, after a while, not for any companies he had worked for but for himself, after he was through with companies taking his ideas and patenting them and giving him credit for the discoveries with pittances and pats on the back. So he had gone out on his own, developed more inventions, garnered his own patents, built three companies and sold them off for what he thought of as huge amounts, and he was right about that. He smiled as he shook his head at the avarice and greed that kept the world of science and business churning away to whatever the future held; and he took his stake off the table and looked for a place to be happy and he had found this place. It cost him a bundle, but he had a bundle and lots more besides, and he bought this place so he could be happy and at peace and it could be a place where the kids and their kids could come back to whenever they wanted, and that was what he got: happiness and peace and security as much as any man could ever want, but it didn't last, because Katy died.

Inexplicably, Katy died. She wasn't supposed to. She was only sixty-eight when they found the thing growing in her, and she had access to the best that healthcare could offer, and they caught it early and said that everything was fine, but it wasn't, and it cropped up in another place, and then another, and another, and they couldn't stop the damned thing with anything, and it was hell on wheels. They went through the same thing that everyone else went through – the running around from clinic to expert to all the best hospitals in the country, then in the world, then in desperation to the craziest of untried, unsanctioned, unsanctified charlatans in every far corner of the globe. No, not just legitimate practitioners unrecognized by the western medical professions. They went to all of those and ran out of them, and then they tried the diets and the chemical cocktails and then they got down to the real charlatans who didn't have anything but twisting words and smiles and their hands out and MacGregor, in desperation, crossed their palms with a lot more than a few pieces of silver, but nothing worked. Nothing. Whatever it was inside Katy, it was eating her alive and it wouldn't stop; and it didn't stop, either, until one morning when he woke up, sitting next to her hospital bed, and she was lying there not breathing and she didn't wake up when he looked at her or spoke to her or put his hand on her shoulder or shook her, and she didn't wake up when the nurses came or the doctors came and they all stood there and looked down at her and tears came to MacGregor and he said barely above a whisper "Oh damn. Oh damn. Oh Katy, my Katy," and it was all over and Katy was gone and what the hell did anything mean any more.

That had been two-and-a-half years ago, in the middle of a deep, bitterly cold and absolutely dreary winter that Katy hadn't been able to face any more of. MacGregor picked up his life and went forward, looking for whatever would mean anything any more, and he was glad that he had the house and the lake and the mountains beyond, for surely they would know something, and they would tell him something, he was sure of that. But they hadn't, yet. They hadn't.

It was past the middle of July, and the kids and their families had descended on him again this year in the middle of June and stayed a month or more, all of the family or big chunks of it all the time or part of the time, and he was glad for that, and happy with all of them around him, galloping through the big house; splashing off the end of the dock into the water; stretched out at the end of the ropes behind the powerful speedboat he called The Champlain Dandy; chomping down incredible amounts of hamburgers and early corn and potato salad and ice cream and soda; watching the sparks fly into the dark night sky from the huge bonfires he built out in the pasture. Far into those summer nights there was laughter and the good healthy growth of strong human bodies and strong memories, too, and that made him glad.

Then they were gone. Maybe he'd see a few of them on Labor Day weekend, and maybe he'd go to one or another of their places at Thanksgiving or Christmas, or maybe if they got really lucky a whole big portion of the tribe would head for a couple or a few weeks somewhere in the tropics or the Rockies in the middle of the winter, something to look forward to, but for right now he was alone, and he didn't mind that. Didn't mind it at all.

He sat on the deck in the middle of the night and sipped his scotch and smoked his cigar and peered across the moonlit lake, and his eyes narrowed as he squinted at the light from a fire over on the far shore. Late for a fire that size so near the shore under the great black looming mass of mountains. Not too many people up this way up so late at night, to have a fire that big blazing away. Too late for graduation parties. Not the solstice. Not the Fourth. All those celebrations gone in the mists of earlier in the summer.

But somebody over there was celebrating. The water was much too wide to hear anything from over there, but something was going on. Maybe someone had dumped some kind of gas or kerosene on the fire at the last minute and made it flare. Dangerous thing to do, but people did it all the time. Then as he watched, and he watched a long time – it was, after all, his lake, and he had to watch over it – the fire began to flicker and dim, and by midnight it was gone, mere coals over there where it had been, and over here, nothing at all remained.

MacGregor got to his feet and walked to the edge of the deck. He sucked on his cigar, made it glow, gathered a good wad of fine brown spit and let it go from between his front teeth in a power stream that sluiced out into the night and settled into the ferns and bracken between the deck and the lake. It startled a big old green bullfrog who was unnerved by this crap landing not three inches from his nose. MacGregor didn't care, didn't even know the frog was there. It looked up at him from twenty feet below, not seeing him, seeing the weather though, wondering where this radioactive, carcinogenic shit had come from. The frog left, even though that place under the ferns had been, until the sheet of brown swill arrived, really sweet with scent and food.

MacGregor turned and walked inside, into the big kitchen where the red 'done' light was lit on the dishwasher. He snickered and turned off the machine, opened the door, looked inside at the one-third filled baskets. "Got away with it again," he muttered. Katy never would have let him get away with that. He couldn't remember how many times he would have the baskets full to overflowing and begin to start that Damned Thing and suddenly Katy would be there, saying, "For God's sake, it's only half full. Get out of the way. Here. Let me get at that."

They could all do that, he knew. Once, visiting his brother-in-law, MacGregor had watched him fill the dishwasher to overflowing only to have his sister-in-law clatter up like a wet hen with an attitude, push the two of them out of the way, and fill the Damned Thing with a third more cups, saucers, plates, utensils, pots and pans and put the soap in and close the door and push the button with a satisfied finger thrust and a look at both of them like they were the worst Neanderthal dolts she had ever encountered. Then she went sashaying away, leaving the two of them to look at each other. "Don't feel too bad, Bob," MacGregor had said. "They can all do it, you know. All of them." Yes, they could all do it. All of them. They had all been waiting four-and-a-half million years for this century to come along, waiting in dark, dank caves while the boys were out whacking things over the head and dragging them to the cave entrance and leaving them there for the girls to cook the stuff and clean up the mess, and the girls had learned over the millennia how to do that just right, so when the dishwasher came along, they knew it was just what they were waiting for, and they had it down pat, sight unseen. No contest. Now go sit by the fire and stay out of the way.

MacGregor snickered again, walked past the machine, put his glass on the table, turned to the refrigerator and popped some new ice cubes into his glass and filled it half full with his second single malt of the evening. Then he meandered out onto the deck again, took a deep, satisfied breath, and started in on the options. The air was filled with options. Stay here. Move to one of those hotsy-totsy senior 'take-care-of-you-for-life-and-even-unto-death' villages up north near Burlington. Sell this place, get a smaller one, or a condo, and foist himself on each of the four kids – a couple of months to each kid – in an unceasing round robin of visits from now until Kingdom Come, or whenever the time came that he'd have to get stuck into a nursing home. Create a scene at one of their homes by crashing to the floor at a Sunday dinner and lying there twitching until the ambulance came shrieking up the driveway. Nah. Not very likely, old bucko. Not for him. Take the Dandy out into the middle of the lake and

jump out of it and try swimming to shore until, exhausted, his
clothes dragged him down to the bottom for the carp to feed
on. God, no. In the summer the water would be too warm; it
would take too long, and God knows what his body would make
his mind feel like by the time that was through. Not in the fall,
either. He'd miss the migrations: the thousands upon thousands
of geese and ducks and blackbirds and warblers and all the
other ones. Wouldn't want to miss that. So leaving the planet
voluntarily was an option, but not one he would ever consider.
Leave that for somebody else to think about. He wouldn't. Life
was too good to let it go without a fight.

So he opted to stay here. This summer he would close up most
of the big house, leave a wing open for himself; then in the
fall he'd move into the smaller guest house. Cozy there. Cozy
enough to sit in and smile and read and listen to the winter wind
roaring off the lake in the night. Cozy enough to come back to
after a morning spent in his workshop in the barn, working like
Santa on the Christmas presents he made for everyone each year.
So much for options. He'd take the last one once again. And
done with them. They bedeviled him every time the kids came
and left, but he'd learned, over the past couple of years, how
to deal with them, and he'd just done it again; dismissed them
summarily. End of that little exercise.

He stubbed out the remains of his cigar and sat down in one of the big heavy Adirondack chairs and looked out over the lake. He took a sip of his Knockando, and set the crystal glass down on the arm of the chair. Quiet. Quiet. Not a sound except the small waves lapping at the shore. Not even the bullfrog chugging away down there in the weeds. Wonder what happened to him. Maybe a heron got him. MacGregor chuckled to himself. Froggie had options too. Maybe one of them got him. Then he saw them.

There were three of them. Three canoes, gliding north. They came around his point of land and struck out for the far shore to the northwest of Buttonmould Bay, keeping to the wide side of Button Island. They came right under him, right past the end of MacGregor's dock. He could only half see them, see the glint of their paddles, the moonlight off the naked backs of the paddlers, the feathers in their hair. The what? Damn. MacGregor reached for his night glasses, then realized they were inside. He bent forward, suddenly wide awake, alert. He watched them silently move across the still waters, heading north.

MacGregor snorted and stared. There were three men in each canoe. Feathers in their hair? Oh, sure. Re-enactors, maybe. There were always people dressing up like…like…but at midnight? Sure. Why not? He watched them as the canoes became smaller and smaller; mere specks in the blue and purple night, farther and farther out on the midnight lake.

And when they had nearly disappeared in the distance, he caught another movement at the edge of his vision, and his eye jumped back down to his dock. Another canoe, and another, came round the point, this time with men in deerskin in them; then whaleboats, dozens of them. He could see the muskets stashed in them. They just kept coming. They came three and four abreast in a kind of loose formation. There must have been a hundred and fifty men in those boats, all uniformed, like the canoeists, in deerskin. More re-enactors? Hell of a lot of them, thought MacGregor. These looked like....like....Rogers' Rangers? What the hell was in this scotch, anyway.

And down from the north, farther out on the lake, came more canoes, with Abenakis and Hurons and Ottawais and Frenchmen in them. MacGregor knew the white men were French because they were singing in French, singing old paddling songs. Up from the south there was another flotilla of canoes filled solely with Indians this time, Mohawks, and they veered to the west and put in on the far shore, the New York shore, and set up camp, and the French and Indians coming down from the north saw them, and headed for them, and a big Frenchman in one of the lead canoes stood half-crouching, holding a big old gun, an harquebus, and he was saying something in French, and the Indians with him were howling and laughing. And MacGregor thought he knew what the big guy was saying: 'Let's see how they like a taste of this baby!' he was saying.

And while the Indians of both camps were setting up on the far shore, up from the south came a French fleet in good array, with what seemed to be thousands of French soldiers cheering and yelling 'Montcalm! Montcalm!'; and from far in the south came the keening of bagpipes, from somewhere near Ticonderoga, maybe it was, and it was a dirge for so many, many Scots dead in a battle of long ago. And as the French fleet disappeared into the north, a shattered flotilla of makeshift boats came scattering down the lake, and behind them was a grand British fleet, driving them all before it, almost catching them, and the rag-tag American fleet made for Buttonmould Bay and their sailors rammed their ships full-speed onto the land and set fire to them. Their American crews came running down along the road, past MacGregor's driveway, running for Fort Independence far in the south, running for their lives, and the British fleet stopped, and waited, and waited too long, and then it was autumn, and the campaigning was over for another year, and the next year was

Saratoga, and the war, although it was not over, was finished, and this was where the Americans had won it.

MacGregor stood by the railing of the deck and stared. He steadied himself, his lean left hand on top of a newel post of the railing. Before him the steps led down to the dock. Beyond that, the lake was as smooth as glass under the brilliant moon. After a long while, he sighed, turned, and walked toward the house. Then he turned again and faced the water. He smiled and said to himself, 'Damn. I'm almost eighty. I'm almost eighty, and nothing like that's happened on this lake in my lifetime. But it all happened. It all happened right here. Yesireebob. God, what a place.' He chuckled, turned, and went inside, well-satisfied with his life and his mind and the state of his imagination.

He undressed and went to bed. And as he lay there, the longing came up once again, tight in his chest, as it did every night. "Good night, Katy-did," he whispered, and he slept.

ACKNOWLEDGEMENTS

I would like to thank all of those who, by their constant encouragement and creativity, have had a part in this endeavor. In particular, I want to thank Donna and John Moody; Marie and Ted Tedford; Jodi Picoult; Jennifer Salmon, our illustrator; and Ann Day and Helen Gow of the League of Vermont Writers. A special Thank You! goes to Pat Goudey O'Brien of Tamarac Press in Warren, Vermont, whose guidance through the publishing world has been invaluable. And another big Thank You! goes to Joan Bowker, with whom I have had the delightful pleasure of being associated since February 14, 1973, when we met in an elevator on the way to the same meeting on the 14th floor of a building on 14th Street in Manhattan. Isn't that somethin'! Oh, and to Buffie, too, who made friends with Donna, who told me the story about dogs.

Underhill
July 10, 2009

Printed in the United States
221670BV00001B/3/P

9 780970 662019